ROUND, THROUGH & OVER

ROUND, THROUGH & OVER

My life as a young sailor in the 1880s

JAMES BARNETT

ISBN: 97987747763719

CONTENTS

PREFACE

James Barnett's journal was discovered in a cellar in Portsmouth in 2014. These surviving fragments provide a vivid portrait of life in the Royal Navy from the perspective of a young sailor in the 1880s.

1

PORTSMOUTH HARBOUR

My story opens in 1884, when Portsmouth harbour truly was a sight to behold.

From Point, Old Portsmouth, looking toward Gosport, just inside and close to Blockhouse Fort, lay the old **St Vincent**, a three-decker and used as a training ship for boys which I hope to refer to again.

Next to meet the eye looking across the harbour was the **Sprightly**, an old paddle steamer used chiefly to bring liberty-men to and from the 'Men-o'-war' lying at Spithead. Next was the **Seahorse**, a smart little ocean tug with double funnels. Both **Sprightly** and **Seahorse** were tied-up to buoys and swinging with the tide, whereas the **St Vincent** was centrally moored bow and stern.

Next came the world-renowned **HMS Victory**, and a couple of cables length further on was the **Duke of Wellington**, and then continuing on the Gosport side of the harbour came a whole string of hulks.

These hulks were mostly Prizes taken from the French. The first was a small, yellow-painted hulk called the ***Tyrian***, which I believe was a very valuable Prize indeed. Then came other and much larger vessels – ***Hannibal***, ***Bellerophon*** (called ***Billy the Ruffian*** by the sailors), ***Boadicea*** and some others.

On the Portsmouth side of the harbour, close to Point, was the entrance to the camber, where our merchant vessels loaded and unloaded their various cargoes. Next came the gunwharf, the pontoon and the railway running into the Royal Dockyard. Then the first glimpse of England's mighty channel fleet lying 'heads & tails' all along the dockyard jetties.

The ***Minotaur*** and ***Agincourt*** were the two outstanding ships, having five masts instead of the usual three. Next was the ***Sultan,*** known to us lads as the ***Turks***. ***Agamemnon*** was another heavily masted vessel, also the ***Lord Warden***, the ***Hector*** and various other 'men-o'war' - all great massive Ironclads. No wonder we lived in peace for years which no doubt was due to our great channel fleet.

Now, if you had time to explore the harbour continuing from the dockyard towards Portchester, you would take a waterman's wherry of which at this time there were plenty. The watermen themselves were grand old salts who would take you to any ship you wished to visit and wait to take you back to the beach again or to any other part of the harbour for 2/- or 2/6d. The wherries were taut little craft brightly painted and with tarred sides. They were quite safe and seaworthy. Many and varied were the names painted on their backboards such as ***Daisy***, ***Beatrice***, ***Sylvia***, ***Florence***, ***Eva*** and many others. The Watermen themselves were very interesting and could tell you everything there was to be known especially about the ***Victory*** and, in fact, any other warship that happened to be in harbour.

Continuing our imaginary trip in one of the wherries from the north jetty in the Dockyard we would pass three more old vessels. The first we come to is the ***Excellent***, then used as a gunnery ship for our naval men. Next, ***Vernon*** - the torpedo school, and the ***Calcutta*** which was used for training artificers and engineers. Some two hundred yards away stands the finest gunnery establishment in the world (Whale Island) where great numbers of our officers and men receive their gunnery training.

This, dear reader, is a brief description of Portsmouth Harbour as I saw it in 1884 when I entered the ***Andrew Miller*** (the Royal Navy). I have up to the present described warships only, but in addition there were a great number of yachts of all sizes and rigs, mostly sailing cutters and schooners. I omitted to say that there was a very good service of ferry steam launches and a floating bridge to and from Gosport.

The writer's intention here is to describe life as he found it, giving names to the ships he passed through, with names of officers and men, whilst describing things that may interest his readers.

I ought to say that previous to joining the RN, I had only seen the sea on one occasion, which was when the rector for whom I worked in 1881 took the choir for an outing from Midhurst to Portsmouth by train. I thought that railway trip from Midhurst to Portsmouth Harbour station was wonderful. We then went by Isle of Wight steamer across to Seaview, and what a tea we had there! It had been a glorious day, but returning home I was late for work next morning.

2

JOINING THE NAVY

My next sight of salt water was early in January 1884 when, to join the navy, I had my second sea trip, this time across the water from Portsmouth to Gosport. The fare was 1 penny but some years later it was actually reduced to ½ a penny. I was directed to the HM Coastguard station, where two burly coastguardsmen rowed me out to the *St Vincent*, or as she was usually called, *The Saint*, where after climbing a steep wooden ladder I entered the side of the ship at the gangway.

I was then taken to the Master at Arms' office where, after giving in our papers and answering many questions, I was taken with four of five other boys to the Sick Bay. Here we were examined by the doctor before being termed New Entries.

On our way to the Sick Bay we had to pass through rows and rows of other boys and the din was beyond description. They were busy as bees laying out their kit for inspection after returning from Christmas leave. They were also engaged in polishing shoes, jack-knives and scissors that had become tarnished, and even rusty, in the salt air whilst their owners were at home. When you consider that the compliment of boys under training on that ship was close to 2,000 you can have some idea of the 'beehive' existence in which we had to live.

After a week or so we New Entries were fitted out with our blue-jacket clothing. Our civilian togs were tied up in parcels and sent to our various next-of-kin. From then on we were considered to be fully blown boy sailors. I don't intend to weary the reader unnecessarily, so I'll only say that during the next eighteen months I had many ups and downs. Needless to say, that time was crammed with every kind of instruction. Sail and boat drills. Rifle, pistol and heavy gun drills – the latter carried out at **HMS Excellent**. Great pinnaces were rowed there and back morning and evening, taking quite a number for heavy gun practice.

3

NAVY FOOD

A few words on the subject of food will now no doubt be of interest.

Breakfast consisted of cocoa, a chunk of bread - to which twice a week a small portion of pig's trotter or knuckle of boiled pork (called 'Bollicky') was added - if you were one of the 'old Joes'. If you had only recently enlisted your chance of getting even a small piece of that was remote. The bread was called 'Scoff'. At dinner, two potatoes and a small bone with little attached meat was known as '2 and a Jonah'. Sometimes we would get pea-soup dinners. Thursdays and Sundays were special days for us and known as 'Figgy-Dowdy' days or 'Gammy and Raisin Duff' days.

For tea we had a small chunk of bread and a 'pannican' of tea. Sometimes there wouldn't be enough to go around so one of the boys was sent post-haste up to the cook carrying a tin kettle to ask for any 'plushers', meaning a little extra. Naval cooks are reputed to be very clean - so much so that they even wash the sugar! The pannicans were little basins made of tin, as were the plates.

Supper consisted of another chunk of bread and treacle was occasionally provided. We called that combination 'basher'. Sometimes a New Entry, when asleep in his hammock, would have a 'basher plaster' pressed over his mouth. This was a piece of sticky-backed brown paper liberally smeared with the black treacle before being applied to the victim's mouth at which time the culprit would swiftly disappear from the scene.

4

NAVY DISCIPLINE

At all times discipline was very strict and punishment for defaulters severe, especially for deserters, those caught stealing and a hundred and one other minor offences for which corporal punishment, stoppage of pay or of shore leave was thought appropriate. Desertion and stealing was punished by birching, and the following is bound to be of interest to my readers.

After a spell of leave, such as summer or at Christmas, two or three boys would for some reason or another fail to return to the ship on time. They were usually brought back to the ship by a police officer, after a few days or weeks of absence. Evidence would then be collected and the culprit brought before the Captain.

The usual sentence was for 24 strokes of the birch to be administered.

At 1130am all boys are mustered on the quarterdeck to witness punishment, and although sixty years have passed by since I stood to watch, I still shudder at the memory and barbarism of the events. A tub of hot water was placed nearby in which were placed two or three birches to toughen them. Each birch consisted of a bunch of birch twigs two and a half feet long and bound tightly from halfway down to form a hand grip. The twigs splayed out from this handle like a besom broom and were soaked in the hot water before punishment began.

The Officers and boys are assembled with the Doctor, watch in hand, available should the victim faint for if this should happen he was to delay the punishment. The victim is then marched between two 'Joeys' (Marines) with a Corporal. The charge is then read out to the assembled company by an Officer who also says what the punishment is to be.

The boy is then lashed over some hammocks already in place for the job. His hands, or rather his wrists, and his legs are similarly lashed together, his back and buttocks bared. A ship's Corporal usually has to do this rotten job. He then takes one of the birches from the tub, shakes off excess water and at a word from the Officer in Charge he starts. SWISH!.....(1) calls the Master-at-Arms. SWISH!.....(2) calls the Master-at-Arms, and so on until twenty-four strokes have been administered, or whatever number had been decreed. After the first four or five, groans of anguish came from the poor youngster as pieces of birch and skin from his now lacerated buttocks and back fly off sometimes onto the faces of the hundreds of boys standing close to witness and be deterred from a similar fate. Sometimes it was only a caning that was administered, but that was bad enough. Quite a batch was lined up for this sort of punishment every day except Sunday.

5

PAY & LEAVE

Pay days were always on a Thursday, when everyone marched past the pay table. Each boy was given either 6d or 3d or classed as N.E. meaning 'not entitled!'

When going home on leave, fares were paid and a few shillings provided to each boy. Luckily some of us had good homes and parents who did all they could to help us spend as happy a holiday as was possible.

I must explain that each boy was actually allowed 3/6d a week, but was only given the amount mentioned earlier - for the rest was stopped to pay for food and clothing, and boys were also allowed to remit a small amount to their parents, which was a very good thing indeed both for parents and boys.

Occasionally, we were treated to a local pantomime, and on one occasion quite a number of the First-Class Boys were taken to an exhibition in London, which we all appreciated very much.

One event stands out in my memory, when some hundreds of us were taken in great launches and pinnaces to Portchester to witness a great review on Portsdown Hill, where thousands of troops were inspected by the Old Duke of Cambridge. The bright colours of the uniforms of the various regiments were a sight to behold. I well remember seeing the Grand Old Duke on horseback with the feathers on his headdress fluttering in the breeze as he took the salute in the great march past. We were supplied with buns and tea and had a real good time for there were roundabouts, swings and various gingerbread stalls, etc.

In the late afternoon, us boys were assembled and marched down the hill to Portchester Castle from where we were to embark in our boats for the trip back to our ship in Portsmouth Harbour. We arrived to find our boats high and dry, for the tide had turned, leaving them stranded on mud flats.

Our instructors were in a quandary as to what to do for the best. The boats would not be afloat again until about midnight, so the Officer in Charge decided to march us all back to Gosport Hard via Fareham, a distance of about fourteen miles. What a march that was. Several boys had to be helped along by others. Some fell-out to take off their shoes and rest before moving on again. A few were refreshed with drinks of water from wayside cottagers. After many hours we did eventually arrive at the Coastguard Station, directly opposite our ship, but what a weary, warn and sad lot we were. Feet blistered and sore for some had been wearing nearly new 'pussers' shoes! I'll leave the reader to try to picture the scene as we scrambled into boats that had been sent for us. Although we had only been away from the ship since early morning, it seemed as if we had been away for ages.

ROUND, THROUGH & OVER

6

SAIL DRILL

I ought now to explain that on Mondays, except for when bad weather prevented it, we were involved with Sail Drill for which everyone in the ship had a station. She was a fully rigged ship and when all sails were set it was a wonderful sight. Hundreds of us were 'running the rigging' and 'manning the yards' to unfurl or furl the great sails. One could write pages on end naming the different ropes and sails and the meaning of nautical terms.

In the rest of the week, one day would be set aside for instruction in 'boxing the compass', with another dealing with anchors and cables. Then, there was time set aside for rifle and squad drill, knots and splices and the hundred and one things that go to make up a sailor's life.

After about a year and three months, all boys are sent off to do their 'brig' training. Each batch has several weeks in these sea-going brigs. I recall two as the **Sea Flower** and the **Martin** - both smart little packets. After a week or so of training, and when the wind is suitable, the cable is unshackled from the buoy and the brig is soon underway, heading for the harbour entrance and bound for Spithead.

What a thrill that was for us all, to see Fort Blockhouse, Southsea, the beach and piers gliding by as we slid through the green water. We had little time to see much for we were all very involved with our stations, trimming sails, etc. We had been at 'sail drill' for some hours when towards evening we dropped anchor at Spithead where we remained until the next day. If the weather had threatened we would have been ordered back into harbour and made fast to the same buoy we had left from.

This routine went on for several weeks, and eventually we were very glad to get back to our parent ship, for life in the brigs was pretty hard, and some of the instructors were not what they should have been. One in particular I'll mention, for he was in the habit of carrying a short length of rope that he used pretty freely but his worst antic was, when 'running the rigging', to come up behind boys with a sail needle between his teeth. This he would stick into boys' buttocks as he came up behind them. He thought this great fun, and little dreamt of the curses heaped upon his head by those who suffered at his hand. Many of them vowed that if they ever met him in the afterlife, he would be paid back with added interest. I wonder if any of them ever had the opportunity. I never saw him again myself.

7

ABOARD MY FIRST SEA-GOING SHIP

After about eighteen months training, boys would be drafted in batches to sea-going ships often for service abroad. One is naturally sorry in a sense to leave one's pals and a ship that has served as home for so long, but the prospect of a seafaring life in a real ship of the line and of seeing foreign lands is a great attraction for every boy.

At last the day came when my name, together with seven others, appeared on the notice board stating that our kit-bags and hammocks were to be ready next day for embarking on the water-tanker *Elizabeth* for we were on draft to **HMS Hector**, the guardship at Southampton Water.

Soon after dinner, the *Elizabeth* duly arrived alongside and when her fresh water had been pumped into the old *Saint*, we boys were told to carry our bags and hammocks on board. Once we had 'cast-off', the ship made its way out of harbour and on to Southampton Water, where after a couple of hours, we clambered aboard the old ironclad, which we thought was to be our home for the foreseeable future.

It was for four of the eight of us but I with three others were soon transported to a Revenue Cutter named the **Frances** 'which had 'hoved-to' in order to pick us up. As the steam launch came alongside the cutter, we were hurried aboard with our bags and hammocks, and were taken below. The sails were then set, and we were paraded before the Captain, where we were told of our duties by the Gunner.

We soon passed Ryde on the Isle of Wight, then the forts were passed one by one till we came to the lightships **Warner** and **Nab**. We headed up channel in a stiff breeze that gradually became stronger, until the little ship seemed to be ploughing through the briny like a torpedo-boat.

We were without steam or engines and were now encountering heavy seas in mid channel. Sometimes the ship would slip gracefully over a wave then down, down into a great trough of angry water before going up, up, before crashing through wave after wave. The ship was 'washing down' fore and aft and, needless to say, we were all soon drenched to the skin. This continued through the night and best part of the next day.

We could get nothing hot to eat or drink. Poor old cook at his stove in the little 'galley' was continually being swamped with salt water. We had to be content with a chunk of bread and a sip of water until the weather moderated and cook made us some cocoa which we were very thankful with. Then came the chance of a wash and the ability to generally sort ourselves out, but it took several days to dry our clothing and bedding.

We were heading for Dover. Our duties there would be various, dealing chiefly with smugglers, lawbreakers and also occasionally moving a Coastguardsman, together with his chattels from one Coastguard Station to another further along the coast, perhaps forty or fifty miles distant. Sometimes we encountered bad weather then I am afraid the bits of furniture and bedding suffered by the time we reached our destination. Sometimes, only the man himself would come having sent his wife and family ahead by train.

I'll try now to give names and descriptions of our Captain and crew. Captain Donald Mclean was a bluff, burly square-shouldered Scotsman with steel-blue eyes. As good an officer who ever wore the two rings and a revenue-cutter man from 'truck to keelson'! Next in command was Mr. Loggett, the Gunner. He was actually a Chief Petty Officer who acted as Chief Steward. Next was the Boatswain, Jim (Jumper) Collins, who was a Petty Officer 1st Class. A big man with a heart as big and kind as is possible for a sailorman to have. I think us boys would have done anything for him no matter how hard the task – and we had some hard times! Next in rotation was Maddocks, or as we called him (Madds). There will be more of him later.

Next came Able Seaman Long (Dodger – for all Longs are called Dodger. He was a seaman gunner and the one to load and fire our little brass 7 pounder cannon when necessary. 'Tubby', the cook, was another Able Seaman then came two Ordinary Seamen whose names were Jack Strop and Dick Stockton. Then us boys, Mickey Breen and Pat Flannagan, who were Irish, George Huggett and me. Together with 'Johnie', the Captain's Steward these people comprised our crew.

I often wished we were back in Portsmouth aboard the old *Saint*, for she didn't roll and pitch about, but as you make your bed so you must lie therein.

8

MY FIRST CHASE

We were on one occasion lying in Dungeness Bay, when our look-out man spotted a French lugger within the three-mile limit which, of course, was strictly forbidden. Our duty was now to capture the vessel and bring her into harbour where the Captain of the vessel would be heavily fined and be likely to have his nets and tackle confiscated. Our Captain gave orders for us to weigh anchor and to crowd on all possible sail as fast as ever we could.

Then came the chase!

No sooner did they spot us hoisting sails than they 'up nets and away', with us following. Our Captain was exasperated because she was showing us a clean pair of heels, and he ordered the 7-pounder to be loaded. 'Dodger' Long first fired a blank charge which had no effect, so he re-loaded with a 7-pound shot. He expertly placed that shot within a dozen yards of the lugger's bow.

THAT DONE IT!

She at once shortened sail, and we came within hailing distance.

Four of us manned a boat and, with the Gunner as Coxswain, we went alongside the craft and brought its Captain back to our ship. On meeting him, our Captain told him that he had been breaking the law and he would be taken to the nearest harbour and brought before a Court. The French vessel followed us like a lamb all the while her Captain was aboard us. We took such people to Hastings or Folkestone where our vessels would be anchored. After the sentence of the Court was delivered, the Captain would return to his ship, which would swiftly disappear in the direction of the French coast.

We often disguised our ship when on the lookout for trespassers. Our little whip-like pennant would be hauled down and, in its place, a Thames Yacht Club pennant would be hoisted. Our White Ensign would be replaced by a blue, or red, ensign turning Her Majesty's revenue cutter into a yacht as far as appearances went. We would then creep up all unawares to a poor Frenchman and catch him on the hop. Sometimes they would try to run for it, but 'Dodger' Long was always ready with his 7-pounder.

Sometimes, just a couple of 'Martini' rifle shots would do the trick, putting bullets through their mainsail. This was often sufficient for they would be unarmed. Our Captain always gave them the benefit of any doubt. After a Captain had been brought to our ship, and with his boat trailing for hours behind us, Donald McQueen would give orders to 'heave-to', whilst the other vessel did the same. We would then return the French Captain to his craft, where he would explain to his crew that he had been let off. This always brought great rejoicing, and on one occasion they then almost swamped our little gig with fish of every description.

When we got back to our ship, we received a good scolding from our Captain, who said it amounted to bribery, and that we should throw the fish overboard. He then discreetly walked away! We did throw a few over the side but the majority went inboard and a glorious 'tuck-in' we had. There was fish for breakfast, fish for dinner and then again for tea.

Our chief difficulty was a lack of cooking oil to fry the fish in. We had them boiled and baked in the oven but, as everyone knows, they are always best when fried. 'Cookie' did his best to overcome the problem by rendering-down some of the ship's Russian Tallow, of which there is always a fair supply in a sailing ship where it is called 'Bosun's Tallow'. It comes as a block of hard fatty stuff, mixed with lime to hide its foul smell. It was used to grease down the mast, and always as we were splicing ropes. It had a dozen and one other uses.

'Cookie's efforts were a failure, for in addition to stinking the living space, to such an extent that we had to run on deck for fresh air, it was truly vile stuff. I am afraid that he spoilt a great dish of excellent fish into the bargain.

Our food generally was scarce, except when we were in harbour at Newhaven, or Dover, where sometimes through severely bad weather we were driven for shelter. These were times we looked forward to.

ROUND, THROUGH & OVER

9

MADDO

The reader will recall that I earlier spoke of Maddo. He was the caterer of the Mess to which all belonged except for the Captain, Gunner and Bosun. These had their own cabin spaces, leaving the remaining ten of us 'messed' together, where we had a reasonable meal allowance to keep us in food.

Maddo, who had the handling of it, somehow or other used to get the Mess money mixed up with his own, and he had that bad complaint we called 'Elbow-itis'. In other words, he was very fond of lifting a pint mug whenever or wherever he had the opportunity. Consequently, our money was often short, and food without it was unobtainable. We all grumbled and the men among us used threats of exposure, but all to no avail. After big rows, he would always promise to make good the losses, but I am afraid the latter was 'pie-crust without filling'.

10

LIFE AT SEA

It was a rough and tumble life at best, and we often had narrow squeaks in the North Sea, where we risked being run down by bigger craft. On one occasion, in a squall, we were in mid-channel when a great fully rigged ship loomed out of the mist and crossed our bow.

We thought our number was up and, just as we were about to crash into her Quarterdeck, a huge wave lifted us up and sideways. Our 'jib-boom' raked his poop, and we dropped just clear of his stern.

What a sigh of relief we all gave.

The Gunner was at the tiller steering with the Captain by his side. I won't relate the language our Captain used toward that particular ship, as kind Providence was watching over us.

All things come to an end, as did out time in the Revenue Cutter **Francis**, but before I leave this stage of my life, I would like to say how good the men on board were to us four boys.

They taught us many practical things that stood us in good stead for years afterwards. We were allowed to take a turn at the tiller when the weather was good and shown how to cut out and make our own clothes. We were also shown the best way to wash them when every drop of water was very scarce and having to be brought from the shore when in harbour. It was kept in wooden barrels called 'breakers' and kept beneath the deck-boards in the lowest part of the vessel.

We were then relieved by four new boys and sent to the mother ship **Hector** again for a few weeks. It was a much quieter life there after the Revenue Cutter experience. We were eventually sent back to Portsmouth Harbour, but this time to the world-renowned **HMS Victory**, where we awaited drafting orders for foreign service. We had a good time on **Victory**, where our chief duties were cleaning and keeping everything shipshape, as there were at this time quite a number of visitors to Nelson's flagship.

I only intend to record the most notable incidents as I saw them. One of these concerned a boy named John Cann. This boy with another whose name I have forgotten were a dinghy's crew. It was just these two boys who took Officers to and from the shore in their little boat. When they were needed the Boatswains Mate, after a shrill whistle, would shout "Away Dinghy Boys!" The lads would then man their boat from the lower boom and come alongside the gangway to take the Officers ashore or perhaps to go to the Dockyard steps to deliver an official letter.

One day the "Away Dinghy Boys!" was heard as usual but only ONE boy turned up. A search was made for the missing boy,

John Cann. He was found down in his mess and ordered to fall in before the Officer of the Day, who asked him why he hadn't manned the boat when it was called away. His reply was that he was not a Dinghy 'boy' for it transpired that the day before he had attained the age of eighteen years, taken before the Captain and rated a 'man'.

The Officer of the Day dismissed him without another word. Before he had time to reach his mess the Officer called the Boatswains Mate to his side and with a twinkle in his eye said: "Call away the Dinghy boy and John Cann, the Dinghy Man". This done the trick, and John manned the boat without a murmur.

The roar of laughter the incident caused was heard throughout the ship and I believe the story is still told throughout the Navy.

ROUND, THROUGH & OVER

11

ABOARD THE TAMAR

Early in May 1886, several of us Boys were drafted to the troopship *Tamar*, a great white and very long ship bound for the China Station.

Before I proceed on that voyage, may I say here what a sight it was in those days to see the great troopships leaving, or returning, from foreign places. I recall the great Indian 'troopers': **Himalaya**, **Crocodile**, **Seraphis**, **Jumna**, **Orontes**, **Tamar** and **Tyne**, and the stores ship **Assistance**.

When any of the 'troopers' came in, or went out, bands in all the capital ships nearby would play them in and out of harbour, as crowds of people, many of them relatives of those on board, lined the piers, jetties and beaches. It was important to get a last look at the outward-bounders, and a first glimpse of the homeward-bounders. What a glorious sight it was, for that latter trailing their long Paying-off pennants, some with a gilded pigs bladder on the end.

The great day came when we too were played out of harbour by the bands and, with last 'goodbyes' said, our hawsers were slipped and our bows tugged clear of the 'Farewell' Jetty by one of the great Government tugs, of which there were three notable ones. These were **Camel**, **Grinder** and **Manly**, the latter being the smallest of the three. They were used for helping, and often saving from accident, the great vessels as they manoeuvred in the close confines of the harbour.

When our ship's head was pointing towards the harbour entrance, our engines began to throb, and soon the cheering crowds and ships bands doing their best to cheer us all up were left behind as we began ploughing the briny.

Our ship was carrying close on 2,000 men and boys. Most were sailors for re-commissioning ships on the China Station, but there were quite a number of soldiers as well. We were bound for Hong-Kong, the first port of call being the lovely Island of Madeira, my first sight of a foreign port.

Our visit was short, with just time for a few of our lads to be fortunate enough to purchase a few pineapples, bananas, etc., before we headed for Capetown and the great Cape Horn, which we eventually rounded.

What weather we experienced there!

Our sails were set to steady her, but we were constantly washing-down fore and aft. The dear old 'TAMAR' got us through it but our sails were nearly blown away. The ship was 'square-rigged' for'ard, and carried quite a large foresail and topsail, both of which were reefed 'close down'. To make matters worse, quite a lot of baggage shifted in the adverse conditions, and this added to our discomfort. When the weather had moderated, the fore hatches were opened, and the baggage was properly re-stowed, which took some hours to do. We were then again on course, and made good progress.

ROUND, THROUGH & OVER

12

TURNING INTO A MAN

I'll not weary the reader by detailing all the ports of call during the voyage, I but will say that during the trip, I eventually arrived at the age of eighteen, when a boy of yesterday becomes a man of today.

Of course I had to pass a test, but it was a simple one really. I was given a length of two-and-a-half-inch rope and told to put a becket, or handle, to a wooden bucket. Besides this task, I was asked by Mr. Lytton, the Warrant Officer Bosun, of the ship we were going out to re-commission, **HMS Heroine**, and several questions about seamanship. My answers must have been satisfactory, for the next day I was taken before the Captain to be rated Ordinary Seaman (O.D.) in the Navy.

With this I was given a man's privileges such as being allowed to smoke with, of course, an increase of pay from 6d per day to 1/3d. Tobacco and a pipe were soon part of my pleasures.

ROUND, THROUGH & OVER

13

SAILING TO HONG KONG

I must now acquaint the reader with the fact that the trip from Portsmouth to Hong-Kong took the best part of three months, for we had to call at several places, and our overall speed was not great.

During our trip, when weather permitted, our Chaplain, The Revd. Mr. Goodenough – a very Godly man – used to hold short services once a week in the Baggage Flat. We used the Sanky Hymns, and bright little services they were too. I well remember how the Chaplain used to talk to us youngsters advising us to keep clear of any dangers that may come our way whilst on the China Station, and I have often looked back to that time with gratitude.

At long last, we entered the land-locked harbour of Hong-Kong, and what a sight met our eyes!

There was the old Depot Ship **Victor Emanuel** laying off the Naval Dockyard, and quite a number of 'men-'o-war' as well as Chinese junks and sampans by the hundred. These crowded around us ready to sell to us every kind of fruit and local wares of every description.

We had not much time for such activity, for most of us were to transfer to the ships we had been sent out to join. Some of them were what the sailors call 'stripped to a gantling', with every rope 'unroven', every yard and mast struck, leaving just the lower yards and shrouds. Living quarters were being re-constructed too so we, whose ships were as described, were put aboard the **Victor Emanuel**, which was to be our home for many weeks, while our own ships were being re-fitted and painted inside and out.

We had to go aboard our respective ships daily as 'working parties'. Some of us wore 'duck' suits, and some were in canvas suits, for we were to do all the dirty work, such as 'rattling down' the rigging, that is fixing the rope ladders to the shrouds, and tarring afresh all standing rigging and stays.

What a time we had working in the boiling hot sun. Tar and pitch was all around us, for the shipwrights were busy putting in new deck planking, as well as splicing together other pieces that had worn thin from much use. There was the smell of boiling pitch as they caulked the new seams, and tar all around us as we rove new ropes in place of old. Finally, we got the spars hoisted into place again. It took many weeks to accomplish all this and for us to be sent from the Depot Ship to our own vessels.

The old **Victor Emanuel** was a homely old hulk and must have been the Hong-Kong Depot Ship for many years. She was alive with cockroaches, some very big, making sailors jump from their hammocks to escape them. As there were no lights to speak of, only small candles, what games the lads would have at night-time! The 'roaches would run over the Mess tables, where some of the biggest would be caught alive, before short pieces of small candle were fixed with hot wax to their backs. Then, with the candle pieces lit, races were run, which was great fun until one night they nearly set the ship on fire. That put an end to this activity!

ROUND, THROUGH & OVER

14

HONG KONG HARBOUR

I ought to give an outline of the great harbour at Hong-Kong.

There are, I believe, three entrances but it appears from inside to be land locked. Facing the town and towering above it is the great Victoria Peak, several thousand feet above sea level. On the left is the notable Happy Valley, where Europeans, and naval ratings, are buried in a large cemetery near to the Naval Hospital. On the opposite side of the harbour lies Kowloon. Further to the west is the firing range, also the entrance to the Canton River.

I often think of Victoria Peak and hear again the boom of a gun and see the puff of white smoke to signal that the mail boat had been sighted. Some hours later, we would see her making for her berth, following which mails were transferred to the Flagship. Soon afterwards, the signal would be made to all ships in the harbour for boats to be sent for their letters. This was a welcome signal for hundreds of us who looked forward to letters from dear ones at home. There were disappointments, of course. Some would sing such songs as

'Have they forgotten me', 'Do they expect me to come?', 'Go then and tell them from me' and 'Write me a letter from home'.

Now for the Fleet: The flagship was the **Audacious**, a masted ship as were most in those days. The fleet consisted of the **Saphire**, **Leander**, **Heroine**, **Satelite**, **Constance**, **Cordelia**, **Espoir**, **Linnet**, **Wanderer**, **Darling**, **Zephire**, and **Merlin**, plus two little gunboats whose names were the **Dee** and the **Don**. This, in those days, was an imposing fleet.

The Admiral would take the greater part of this fleet of ships for a northern cruise to 'show the flag' in both China and Japan. For many of us, this meant a starvation trip. As we could not procure fresh bread, we were on 'hard tack' - sometimes black with weevils. For dinner, we were given salt horse, pickled pork or pea soup.

One of our worst troubles was fresh water.

We were often very short, for the rudimentary condensers were not at their best in those days, often breaking down completely. Supplies were cut to a minimum, and the scarce drinking water was brackish. Water tanks were under lock and key, and there was an allocation of only half a pint or so per person.

Washing clothing was a real problem. Sometimes tropical downpours would provide us with a real treat. I've seen many of our lads washing as they let the rain drench them. I am, of course, speaking of leisure hours, not during working or drill time. I have run many a time with a bucket and begged for an Officer's bath water from his marine servant, so that I could use it to wash my clothes. He would otherwise have thrown it down the chute.

We were sometimes able to get some fruit from the Chinese 'bum-boats' fairly cheap in the ports we visited. Generally, we were glad when the cruise came to an end, and we were once more back in one of the big harbours such as Yokohama, Kobe, Nagasaki, Shanghai or Hong-Kong, where we would be able to get fresh meat, eggs, bread and fresh water from shore.

15

ABOARD THE HEROINE

Our ship, the **Heroine**, was barque-rigged, so we had plenty of work with the sails, often stopping the engines to rely entirely on the sails when there was a good breeze. Our Captain, C J Balfour, was a very small man and rather quiet for a sea captain. Our 'Number One', W G White, was well built and virtually ran the ship unaided. He was, I believe, as good a sailorman as ever commanded a ship. The rest of the Officers were quite a decent lot, and the men made up a fairly happy crew, even though we had some fairly rough times together. At our church services, we had a notable 'Blue' Marine (Royal Marine Artillery) who accompanied on a small portable organ. His name was Wellington but, of course, he was always called 'Duke'.

Concert parties were special occasions when in harbour. We were allowed this exceptional treat with invitations for a limited number of men from other ships in harbour invited on board. The entertainment was a credit to the artistes, because all necessary rehearsals were done in their own time when off duty. The songs, sentimental and comic, were often quite up to date. I call to mind one of the latter sung by 'Perky', a great raw-boned Able Seaman named Perkins. It ran like this:

> *One caught a <u>louse</u>,*
> *Another said: "Let him <u>loose</u>.*
> *Knock him down with a goose*
> *Another said: "Darn his eye,*
> *For 'tis my Lady's holiday"*
> *So let us all me merry*

Then there were all sorts of 'sing, song' evenings which passed many happy hours away.

We had a dog belonging to the Captain, and a black billy-goat that had been turned over to us from the crew of the earlier commission. 'Billy' originally came from Robinson Crusoe Island and liked it best if he could catch one of the lads bending down and facing away. He would take a few paces backwards and stand briefly on his hind legs before head-butting the bending one. This caused no end of fun. He was not particular regarding food and would eat tobacco leaves, paper as well as emery cloth.

Sometimes while 'Sails', the sailmaker, was stitching away at a canvas, Billy would creep up behind him and get the end of twine between his teeth. He would then commence to chew, and the twine would unwind from the spindle. This would continue until 'Sails' turned to re-thread his needle, by which time 'Billy'; would have consumed yards and yards of the twine. Then there were ructions, with 'Sails' trying to recover most of his precious twine from the animal's tummy, the goat having retreated to the far side of the ship to avoid capture by pursuing sailors armed with mallets and belaying pins.

We lost poor Billy one cold winter, but he was by then a good age. He had been a great favourite with the crew and after he had died an Officer had Billy's head stuffed and set into a frame!

We also had a few birds and monkeys with us. Our sister ship, the *Satellite*, even had a young black bear as the ship's mascot. We had a fairly happy commission, with few serious accidents until we were homeward bound. We were on shore at a port of call engaged in field-gun exercises, when one of the gun team was knocked down with the gun carriage wheels passing over his legs. 'Knobby' Clark was his name, and he was on the sick list for months thereafter. Then, we had a man who had a bad fall from 'aloft' but fortunately his injuries were not fatal. On the journey home, we lost one man through 'spar drill,' when one of the top-gallant masts came crashing down right on to poor Patsy Ryan, who lingered for a couple of hours before dying. We buried him at sea, sewed-up in his hammock, with two round-shot at his feet. It cast a gloom over the whole ship for days.

Not long after this sad event, our Captain's coxswain was lost overboard. Our sea-boat was launched, and the area searched, but no trace of poor 'Taff' Hicks could be found, so there were sad moments during our home-coming.

Overall, the trip took us a couple of months, for we had to 'coal-ship' at various ports on the way.

We came via Columbo, Aden, The Red Sea and Suez Canal. Our trip out in the **Tamar** had taken us round Cape Horn, but now we were to return by the other available route. We were bound for Devonport, where our ship was to 'Pay-Off'. We arrived there in due course with our pennant flying.

There followed many weeks of slogging, as we dismantled all parts of our ship, and returned ropes and stores of every kind to Dockyard Stores. This included all sails, ammunition, etc., until the ship was just an empty hulk. In the ordinary way, the ship's company should have been granted seven weeks leave, but as the great mobilization of just about every sea-going ship available was commencing, we were packed on board them for manoeuvres that lasted for two months!

We were all very disappointed at not being able to go to our homes as hoped for.

To make things worse we were split up from colleagues with whom we had sailed the world to join different ships. I, with a number of others, was sent to the cruiser **Undaunted**, and what a wretched time we had there. Everything was upside down, dirty and begrimed, for she was just out of Dockyard hands. The captain and commander were not too bad, but we were all very thankful when these exercise manoeuvres were over, and we were sent off to our homes for eight weeks and two days well-earned leave.

It was a queer feeling when parting from each other after the four years we had been together without seeing our families. You may meet a few of them again on return from leave, but for the most part, they were gone from your life forever.

I, with a number of fellow A.Bs, was to return to the old ***Duke of Wellington*** some to await dispersal to other ships.

16

HMS EXCELLENT

I was among those who applied for **HMS Excellent** to undertake a course in gunnery.

The old ship was lying between Whale Island and the Dockyard in Portsmouth, and had been the Navy's Gunnery School for many years but now, in 1889, a new Whale Island Gunnery Establishment was being built. As soon as the first block of buildings were ready for occupancy my class of twenty was transferred ashore to A1 Block. Having commenced my gunnery training in the ship I finished it, after several months, at Whale Island.

Although it meant a lot of cramming and study, these were some of the happiest times for many of us, for everything, the result of strict discipline, happened just like clockwork. You knew exactly what you had to do, and when done your time was your own.

The accommodation was very comfortable and, in my opinion, **HMS Excellent** was the finest establishment in the world for sailormen.

Our class instructor was Dan Higgins. We called him Dan 'Leno' after the famous actor. He was a real good sort, as were all of our instructors, all good seasoned sailormen, petty officers and chief petty officers. I recall the old Drill Shed, where the Chaplain conducted a short morning service every day except for Saturdays. One verse of one of the hymns was:

> *New every morning is the love,*
> *Our wakening and uprising prove,*
> *Shake off dull sloth and joyful rise,*
> *To pay the morning sacrifice.*

After the usual prayers, the classes were marched off, accompanied by the fife band, by their various instructors. I well remember those happy days and recall with pleasure my fellow trainees of the time.

At the end of the Gunnery Course, I was drafted to Sheerness Barracks in Kent as an A.B. Instructor to the New Entry 2nd Class Stokers. The following week, my brother-in-law was also sent there. There were six of us Able Seaman and one Chief Petty Officer who was actually our 'boss'.

This proved to be a very good job for me to have, for I was soon able to be joined by my wife and for us to live in a small house.

My duty was chiefly to drill the young stokers before they were eventually sent to ships.

On one occasion, the Officer of the Day, while doing 'rounds' of accommodation, saw that one of the sailor's white straw hats had been left on the 'Crawfoot'. He stood still and looked at it, and then said to the ship's Marine Corporal, standing alongside him and carrying the lantern, as was customary: "Well, in all my naval career and experience, I've never before seen a white hat stand the Rounds!"

On another occasion, the same officer, again doing the 2100 rounds of living spaces, saw a sailor's ditty box left by mistake on the mess table. He ordered the Master-at-Arms to take the box and to lock it - but to put the key inside for safety!

One sad thing I must report is that when my brother-in-law and I were cleaning a 7-pounder gun, placed in the quadrangle for drill purposes, an accident happened. Somehow, as he was about to lift the breech of the gun, I pressed the muzzle down. Neither of us realized what might happen, and sadly the first finger of his right hand was trapped and the top was cut off. I nearly fainted but he bravely didn't make too much of it - but it put him on the sick list for about a week.

ROUND, THROUGH & OVER

17

TURNING INTO A LEADING SEAMAN

After a further eighteen months, I was made Leading Seaman for which I was very proud and thankful.

This meant another draft chit and shifting our home to Portsmouth. I was soon moved again, however, this time to the *Tyne* troopship that took us to Halifax, Nova Scotia, where after a day or two we, with three other ship's companies entrained with the great Canadian Pacific Railway Company for the overland journey to Vancouver, British Columbia.

Now instead of waves we had the rolling prairies, creaking bridges over rivers, the Devil's Dyke and all the wonders of Canadian lakes and forests.

Sights and sounds to last a lifetime

oooOOOooo

ROUND, THROUGH & OVER

ABOUT THE AUTHOR

Little is known of James Barnett, who was born in 1868 and died in 1950.

Martin Hoskins, who has abridged his journal, was educated at the Royal Military Academy, Sandhurst, Brunel University and the State University of New York. Martin's books include 'How to be a Decent DPO: letters to aspiring privacy pros' and 'From Fear to Hope: the story of the early years of the Terrence Higgins Trust, the UK's first HIV/AIDS charity.'

Printed in Great Britain
by Amazon

71960178R00037